The Economy of the future

THE EVOLUTION OF CONSCIOUSNESS

By:

Maria Alexandra Suárez Ríos

ECONOMY FOR PROSPERITY AND EVOLUTION EPE

PEISH® Methodology

The Economy Of The Future, "The Evolution Of Consciousness"

Author: Maria Alexandra Suárez Ríos
Economy for Prosperity and Evolution EPE.
PEISH ® Methodology

Collaborators:
Content editor: Monica Mendieta
Style editor: Silvia Vanegas de Arciniegas
Graphic design:
Front picture: María Alexandra Suárez Ríos

Editorial: Independently Published; 1er edition (26 November 2020)
Publication date: 26 November 2020. ASIN: B08P6JKPSR
ISBN-13: 979-8597479866

First edition in Colombia: December 2020.
Bogotá, Colombia. Edition and printing:
Nit.: 900392296-9 Autores Editores SAS-
Diagonal 36 bis #20- 70, Bogotá, Colombia.
ISBN 978-958-49-1460-6 Printed in Colombia

©All rights reserved

The economy studies how to lead us to greater well-being; however, if we want our humankind to exist and remain, we must think about evolving and increasing our consciousness level.

Maria Alexandra Suarez Rios

This book is dedicated to all of us who think that consciousness's evolution has something to do with earthly life and changing the world. Only a leap in consciousness and responsible actions will lead us to a prosperous future.

To my mother, being she the inspiration of my way of life, to Stella Ríos de Suárez for teaching me: *"That everything is possible"*.

To my family, my father, my brother and sibling, my nephews, and brothers-in-law, thank you for always encouraging me.

And especially to my husband for his unconditional support and to my son, who is living love.

María Alexandra Suárez Ríos

TABLA DE CONTENIDO

THE ECONOMY OF THE FUTURE "THE EVOLUTION OF CONSCIOUSNESS"..12

PREFACE: 14

1   THE ECONOMY OF PROSPERITY AND THE EPE EVOLUTION 21

   1.1   The EPE model..21

   1.2 What we are looking for..36

2   EVOLUTION 40

   2.1   Evolutionary growth through spiritual growth or the understanding of evolution 43

   2.2   The importance of personal and spiritual growth for society ...47

   2.3   Ego and Being..50

   2.4   Correspondences 57

   2.5   Evolution 60

3. NEW EARTH 63

   3.1. Women as an evolutionary factor 63

   3.2. Childhood is a treasure. 79

      3.2.1. THE FUTURE IS ADULTS' RESPONSIBILITY 86

   3.3 Prosperity and old age..89

   3.4 Changes in the Economic Approach 94

   3.5 Leading from consciousness..99

Bibliography 103

Other titles of the author: 105

THE ECONOMY OF THE FUTURE "THE EVOLUTION OF CONSCIOUSNESS"

By: Suarez-Ríos, Maria Alexandra

To evolve towards the economy of prosperity will allow for more significant equality, well-being, and prosperity in society, based on creating awareness and establishing the basis for building policies and actions that will lead us to be a more family-friendly and equitable country. Inspired by promoting the creation of an economy more responsible with planet earth and seeking to be sustainable, I have a proposition: to leave the era of the Ego and individualistic actions behind. We must move on to create an era of evolution based on all human beings' spiritual growth so that our specie ceases to be just a specie located at the first levels of consciousness. The spiritual awakening must be able to permeate the economy and the way we relate to each other.

Herewith, we are betting on a substantial change; a change that leads us to be a species that seeks and promotes peace and prosperity, in which egos do not rule the destiny of the planet. Let us succeed in creating a path supporting individuals and families as the central axis of sustained and sustainable development.

This is the way I see life: uniting economy with spirituality and with human growth, by creating a higher level of consciousness. It is a gift of life to be an economist and a humanist and, even more, from a holistic vision, being able to create spaces to change the reality for all people.

KEYWORDS: Equity, families, economy, prosperity, well-being

Preface:

Economics and spiritual growth seem to be two very different and dissimilar trends. However, both economics and spiritual growth seek to base the development of societies with the resources we have to create prosperity. Therefore, it is imperative to show the world a new way of conceiving society's growth. We could part from a model that integrates the role of women in an equitable and egalitarian manner. A model based on families as the nucleus of society, where the elderly is respected, their wisdom is valued, and we all live in harmony with nature.

The inequity that has been generated by the way women have been treated along history and now at her workplace has led society to have significant problems on the educational and family level. This situation has impacted the purchasing power, consumption, investment, and disharmonized family nuclei, affecting the relationship between family, business, education, and the State itself.

Under different academic proposals and studies worldwide, it has been evaluated that women have a fundamental role in the economy and society. Parting from this conclusion, we can give a new approach to achieve greater well-being in the Colombian economy and create prosperity from exploitation of the resources we have in our society.

Given the moment and the country's and the world's situation, it is essential to create a different society. We need to create a more family responsible society, taking it as the pillar to improve health, equity in all senses and all social agents. This Model would be based on consumption and investment from the Economy of Prosperity Model, which generates greater evolution and growth.

The Economy of Prosperity and Evolution (EPE) model seeks to create awareness and the basis for establishing policies and actions that allow for greater consumption, more significant investment, better health indicators, and the provision of opportunities. This Model should optimize our children's cognitive and emotional development, establish the basis for a different way of doing things, build fairness without going to extremes, to provide guidelines for a change based on women, family, and prosperity for a country.

Another necessary milestone in this approach is the change of focus in education and school system models. Teaching today is conceived as the transmission of knowledge. Still, it is a complex and dynamic activity determined by the local, regional, national or international environment. In their teaching work, teachers almost always guide and transmit, implicitly, the values and rules that are part of the knowledge itself (Granés, 1998). Teaching must be undertaken as a reflective practice through which power can be socialized, made explicit, shared, distributed, and transferred without inequality.

For this reason, this proposal seeks to develop the Economy of Prosperity and Evolution Model (EPE. It aims at increasing welfare from equality by improving the use of resources and agents that exist in the economy, to create an impact on families, businesses, education, health, and government, being responsible with the development of the family and promoting, in a unique way, the economic equity in the working world among all its participants.

This proposal explores the theoretical basis for validating the hypotheses, and their formulation will be carried out. The Model will then be formulated, measurements and statistical reviews will be made, and transparent policies and actions will be proposed to articulate the Model with the economy and reality. The aim is to find a way to build equity and prosperity in society, rather than wealth itself.

Equality towards women allows to create a leap in the social, cultural, and economic development of a country, allowing to generate a healthier, fairer society, capable of producing answers to the country's needs, being socially sustainable, and familiarly responsible. It is expected to increase welfare from equity by improving the use of resources and agents in the economy thus impacting families, businesses, education, health, and government.

It is necessary to formulate clear public policies to achieve gender equality, family, health - breastfeeding, enterprises and companies, employability, remuneration, and a retirement pension model from the EPE impacting families, businesses, and the State. So, to provide an economic model that generates an impact on creating equality within society and respect for families as the fundamental nucleus, will lead us to highlight women and their role in society. It will allow us to build the foundations to develop family, responsible businesses and create policies to generate greater welfare for families and, in the real economy, from responsible consumption to new forms of employment.

What am I aiming at with this book?

- To build alternatives that allow new social change opportunities, understanding that the family is the most important nucleus of society in which women are the natural axis. Therefore, all aspects of growth and prosperity will be favored, with gender justness and equality, familiar psychological health and support for a dignified old age, through the Economy of Prosperity and Evolution Model.

- To provide a new way of thinking parting from the proposed Economic Model to increase labor and economic equality for women in today's society.

- To generate an impact on defining differently evolution and prosperity, integrating spiritual growth as a tool for economic growth to create sustained development.

- To provide a model to start working from the academy and towards the real world, in recognizing the family as the most important nucleus of society, companies, the State and, in general, all economic agents, contributing to build a childhood full of opportunities.

To develop this Model and explain its approaches, I am going to explore a broad theoretical framework. The theoretical foundation begins with the definition of the economy and the creation of wealth in society. It then discusses topics such as the theory of female's consumption in society and economy, the importance of women in infants' development, the impact of extended breastfeeding on health, and public economies. I will propose to explore child and cognitive development, the advantages of breastfeeding, women's cognitive abilities, and how they differ from men.

I will also go deeper into the existing wage differences between men and women, women's productivity levels, the importance of a retirement pension at the end of working life, a dignified old age and the adult and elderly population's valuation. Likewise, I will explore the development of children and the importance of the family within it, family as the nucleus of society, family-conscious businesses, evolutionary growth through spiritual growth, and the importance of personal and spiritual growth for humanity. Although there are many topics, each one is linked to a part of the Model.

1 THE ECONOMY OF PROSPERITY AND THE EPE EVOLUTION

1.1 THE EPE MODEL

Economy studies how to increase the well-being of society by managing scarce resources. Different economic models seek to review the impact of each of the variables involved in the economic models and how each one of them explains society's growth. As human beings advance and technological developments and advances change how we relate to each other, laws are modified. Philosophy shows us the need to include new variables in economic models. With capitalism being the foundation of the financial relationship of many economies around the world; however, the economic agents and variables that are added, go beyond wild capitalism.

In economy, we see the relations of the different agents that intervene in it: The State, companies, individuals, organizations, the internal and external productive sector, as well as the various economic processes, among others, the elaboration of raw materials, manufactured goods, machinery, services and infrastructure. Understanding each of the economic agents' interactions and how they influence the analyzed variables is an exciting exercise because it shows the "cause and effect" relationship.

The PEISH® Model starts from an economic model and explains the importance of working on the human species being the focus, that is, on each person, to achieve social welfare and growth towards prosperity. To this end, the following definitions and postulates are proposed:

The economy studies how to create wealth, and this is where, by relating the economy to evolution from personal growth to reach a higher level of consciousness, the definition of wealth is changed and postulated: To change wealth for prosperity and/or abundance. It is then, to propose that Economy study how to create a prosperous society that maintains a sustained growth to reach a community where the basic needs are satisfied and, and, that Economy think about how to gain the capacity to assign to consumption the way to generate greater well-being, that is transformed in greater comfort and even, in necessary aspects to leave the process of "only survival".

Following the above, income will be equal to consumption, investment, savings, less taxes, and less debt.

$$Y = Cm + Inv + Sv - debt$$

Consumption is the value that households or individuals make in the exchange of currency or means of exchange to obtain or cover their basic needs, more goods, more services, less credit, more luxury, and more investment.

$$Cm = BN + Go + Serv - Cre + Lux + Inv$$

These basic needs are the necessary consumptions that an individual must make to achieve a minimum satisfaction in his life's quality, that is to say, that moves him away from poverty. It is necessary to live without worrying about the deterioration of our life possibility. For this reason, from the perspective of well-being, I formulate it as to be able to cover food (Fo), education (Ed), housing (Ho), public services (Ps) (water, light, sewage, garbage, electricity, or gas), clothing (Cl), transportation (Tr) and health & pension (H&P).

$$BN = Fo + Ed + Ho + Ps + Cl + Tr + H\&P$$

This definition is slightly different from the standard definition of basic needs because I included health and retirement pension variables. I am herewith establishing that they are vital for a minimum quality of life and housing, essential clothing, and food with minimum food standards for not living with malnutrition or be in indigence. Understanding goods as movable and immovable property as car or means of transportation, beds, televisions, cell phones, dining tables (table and seats), living rooms, dishes, cutlery, and kitchen items.

$$Go = \Sigma\ B1\ldots\ldots Bn$$

And when talking about services, I include additional services that add quality of life or greater comfort, such as prepaid or private health services, television cable or private telephone, internet, and travel services.

Serv Health plus + TV serv + Celph + Internet + Travel +oth

I include those paid with the financial banking system and those spent with the non-banking financial system in credits. For example: cooperatives and associations at the legal level.

Cr=BankSys+Coop+Associations

In investments, those consumptions are made in personal property other than housing use, i.e., programmed savings, CDT's (fixed term investments), shares, stock market positions, etc.

Inv=BM+Cdts+Act+StockMk+Other

The variable "luxuries" includes all consumption that is part of purchases in goods and services that generate greater comfort but are not necessary. It also happens in terms of the high acquisition capacity of individuals. They are used to show a higher purchasing level, such as luxury cars, watches, exclusive trips, club memberships, magazines, payments of luxury restaurants, etc.

$$Lux = B1 + Blux2 + ... + Bluxn$$

However, there is a supply and demand for goods, services, and credits. Each individual's request depends on his income plus his ability to pay for goods and services. Now, the family demand will depend on the income of the individuals that constitute the family and the sum of their ability to pay or their possible level of debt, in the future.

$$Demand = Inc - PayCap$$

The companies' production capacity will give the supply, the government and the agents that intervene in the internal economy, including imports and subtracting exports.

$$Off = Go + Serv - Exp + Imp$$

The country's wealth will be dictated by the capacity of the government, companies, and people to generate the prosperity the country needs. Each agent will offer and demand something. However, it is imperative to recognize that individuals receive a salary given by their capacity to generate that economic dimension. It translates into their ability to monetize their skills and knowledge through their trade.

Individual = Economical Dimension

= Monetizing Capacity

(Abilities + knowledge − fears − defects)

This personal dimension grows from acquired knowledge, the values and behaviors learned from authority and affection during childhood, and the lived experiences that remain installed as skills and knowledge acquired through their trade.

Economical Dimension (Personal Dimension)

$$= \sum \text{personal dimension of n individuals}$$

Companies invest in their educated individuals and generate knowledge, which brings them closer to satisfying basic needs from real wealth, which is prosperity and not accumulation.

Personal dimension =

(Learned values

± authority and affection behaviors

± life experience ± knowledge

Net profit can be invested in accumulating or generating prosperity. This proposal applies to the financial system, government, businesses, and the economic agents to create wealth and prosperity. If we imagine a government that, rather than being protectionist, design, and support policies so that basic needs included secondary education for all, efficient transportation systems, health coverage and retirement pension systems, generation of quality public services, access to drinking water and sanitation, wealth would not be thought of as a luxury, but as a way to materialize prosperity.

The materialization of prosperity in individuals happens through individual daily work. They can monetize their skills, knowledge, experiences, and behaviors to reach the minimum consumption level so to cover their basic needs. Afterwards, the remaining items of the Model can be included. Because individuals are responsible for their own lives, the external results will be low if they do not work on their interior power.

If individuals are part of companies, the government, and other economic agents, we must support the individual and the companies so to understand that what they do is not complying with a contract. It is an exchange of dreams between parties. Organizations hire individuals to achieve a vision or a goal (a reason for being). The individuals employed, in exchange, materialize their dreams with the income they receive, with the development and their performance within the environment (we return to our consumption equation).

Thus, the sum of individuals' work will allow or generate the organization to achieve its dreams. In return, the organization will give individuals the ability to achieve the desired consumption level and professional fulfillment so that they manage to develop as people aligned with their personal lives. In other words, the PEISH® Model is born by integrating the needs of individuals with organizations' needs to generate a more prosperous society.

The economy agents are made up of institutions, organizations, government, State, industry, economic sectors, among others. Each one of them is build up by people. The vital element for the institutions' survival (State, private, public, associative, cultural companies, among others) and the generation of the dynamics and interactions in the economy and society are the people. Therefore, people and everything that happens inside these entities are the fundamental basis of our analysis.

However, do not forget that organizations are conformed by people, and each person is part of a family. Therefore, the theory stating that families are the most important nucleus in society must be strengthened due to the emotional, economic, and financial, psychological, social, environmental, and educational stability.

Institutions Entities, enterprises, etc. $= \sum n \, people$

People are part of families

families (grandparents, mothers, children, pets)

We propose then the Economy of Prosperity, which seeks to generate development and evolution through the growth and evolution of four (4) main variables: 1) The role of women; 2) Childhood as a treasure; 3) The family as the central nucleus of society, and 4) A dignified old age.

SUPPOSITIONS:

Let us suppose that by modifying the great majority of people's personal dimension from a holistic and more spiritual approach, we can lead society to create a more prosperous society.

Many people ask what I mean by this statement. The personal dimension depends on the values we have learned and the behavior we assume. We integrate this behavior as we grow up, especially in our childhood; those prior experiences respond to the relationship we have forged with our parents. Therefore, our children's immediate environment or our nations' children depend on what they learn from adults. The answer to transforming society lies in changing adults' behavior to achieve a healthier childhood in each country and nation.

Adults' responsibility towards the future of the planet is and means everything. However, each of these adults works in a business environment to materialize and obtain their livelihood resources, leading them to interact with all economic society agents.

In this sense, the future of our planet depends on labor and business relationships. These relationships are largely impregnated by a game of egos and roles that lead society to compete for more physical wealth, leaving aside our spiritual growth or evolution as humankind.

The institutional and productive world is a predator of families and, in many cases, the main reason for abandonment during childhood. Family members walk away to fulfill a series of activities, knowing that no one is indispensable in life. Any human being can be replaced immediately. The family, being destroyed by emotional and affective abandonment, can suffer long term consequences.

The little awareness of the importance that childhood receives in the family as an essential nucleus, of women's need for equality as the axis of change and respect and, the appreciation of old age, leads the human species to a constant destruction of the capacity to evolve and maintain ourselves as a species.

Much is said about spiritual growth and even happiness as isolated factors in the economy. But for a minute, let's think about what would happen if we included the variable of spiritual growth or consciousness development in the Model. The personal dimension would change, impacting the Model from each person's inside.

Personal dimension=¿

+spiritual growth or consciousness evolution

It would lead society to work and allocate great resources to foster respect for one another and understand childhood as a vital factor in our species' evolution by grounding Ego and Being's concepts, it would be possible to realize that the economic and material end is not what prevails in developing our race, society, and humanity.

We all must expand consciousness to understand that the correspondence towards destruction is given due to egos' fight for power and money.

And in that sense, we allow ourselves to see that the other human being, whatever race he or she may belong to, has a passing through Earth with a purpose beyond hoarding money and power. And none of these things can be carried to the next life (if there is any).

Let us imagine we are part of a society that parts from respecting all, without extremism, such as wild capitalism where only economic power prevails, or irrational socialism where everything is "free" (total paternalism of the State). Instead, we build companies with social, family, and ecological awareness, which allow us to have limits, to achieve respect for all economic agents and to search for sustainable growth. In this way, we will be on Earth taking care of scarce resources, many of which are not renewable. We will then have a different planet.

The Colombian journalist Guillermo Latorre, known as "Pirry," said: "I still do not know another planet to which we can move to. Although many businessmen and many people do ecological damage, I still do not know how we will manage it. Have they already got another planet to move to? And if it is true, as soon as we destroy everything in our path, nothing will change if we as adults don't change our ways."

And we do not have to wait for future generations. We have to start with us, those in your 70's, 60's, 50's, 40's, 30's, 20's, with everyone. The Ego of each one of the businessmen, of the parents, of the teachers and of society itself is so high that irrational competition for power will lead us to the destruction of towns, cities, families, children and of human existence.

1.2 WHAT WE ARE LOOKING FOR

Because I studied economics and many other subjects of transpersonal psychology, theology, religions, Magic of

Love School, postulates of emotional intelligence and the multiple intelligences, cognitive development, education, taxonomies of learning, personal and family healing, art, painting, and singing, I manage to see the precise relationship between the spiritual, the evolutionary dimension and the development of societies. With this Model, I seek to generate a bridge between the economy and the spiritual growth or the development of conscience, from that essential point: family. For me, the relationship between childhood and adult behavior is evident. If we adults do not behave as such, that is to say, that we protect family, youth, elders, and each of our community members, we will continue to destroy what is vital in society: people.

It is also obvious to me that companies have to be aware of the role they play in society. If the manager, boss, or director in a company is not aware of his impact on the families of those who work there, the future will be at risk. Even from his unconsciousness, he affects his employee or collaborator's evolutionary development and, also, his children. The impact on children is the cost we are paying as society with the irrational race of Egos to possess objects, hoard money, finish with the planet, build empires lacking of evolutionary reasons, leading to the creation of very light and nonfunctional societies, from evolution's perspective.

We must stop and ask ourselves as a human species: ¿Where are we going? ¿How sustainable is it for the human species to destroy itself through the wars of the Egos?, Are the wars that our ancestors have lived through, not enough?, What is the purpose of destroying the others?

There is a song by Amaia Montero that states a precious phrase for my analysis: *"The smallest life is worth a thousand times more than the biggest nation."* Paradoxically, nations have felt the right to destroy the lives of millions of people, just because of the illogical fight of the human's Ego, so to have and own land, power, money and everything that leads to accumulation and generating high profits, no matter what families or people perish as a result of it. Consequently, we lose the reason and vision of all as a species that walks through finite human existence. And at the end of the road, no one who has treasured wealth takes anything away.

I seek to generate some awareness in the way we plan our economies. Giant steps have been taken towards formulating international policies that respect human rights, spaces for the caring protection of the planet, campaigns to support children, equality, equity, etc. Nevertheless, we still lack much evolutionary awareness about the need to manage from our primary emotions to the most destructive behaviors. The Ego is the big winner, and our human species is the loser. It loses lives, families, and children; that is, destruction ends up being the way of society nowadays.

The fight against violence begins with children's care, with adults' support encouraging them to be responsible. With the forgiveness process, we all need to respect the other one, with mental and emotional health support, allowing families to build a more harmonious and loving society. The fight against all types of crime is not punishing the crime itself; it is in families' development, respecting human existence, putting aside the uncontrollable desire to have so much that it will never fill the heart. All material things do not replace affection that was lacking during childhood. Every adult has a story of his childhood and many things to heal since then.

As human species, we must stop the massive destruction, hatred, excesses and instead, walk harmoniously as a species. But this is not achieved if we do not reach a higher level of consciousness. To reach that higher level of consciousness I am talking about, we must work on each one of us, on that personal dimension that leads us to build a new world in our mind and even in how we materialize our evolution harmonized prosperously with society and the planet.

2 EVOLUTION

When I speak of evolution, I am talking about the capacity we have as individuals to build within us the necessary conditions to live together in harmony, seeking for our planet's well-being and prosperity, based on respect for human existence in all of its expressions and forms, without exclusions. The most evolved person is the one who respects and understands differences as a natural expression of existence and builds agreements to solve all he cannot understand or with what his beliefs cannot coexist.

Evolution is the very expression of controlling the Ego, understanding emotions, healing the primary manifestations of absence or lack of authority and affection in childhood, and the cognitive capacity to build new forms of expression, even if we do not agree with each other.

Suppose we manage to banish from our mind, as human species, the need to finish or eliminate others because they do not think or are, as we want them to be. We will then be able to inhabit a planet that seen from outer space does not have borders and understand we are beings with different physical manifestations. Although we have a short life experience (between 0 and 100 years), we can reach something different from treasuring money, land, and objects.

Evolution is: being able to live in peace. A peace that comes from within each person, with absolute respect for the other and understanding that we all are valuable. By making agreements, we can stop the destruction of the species and the planet.

Evolution implies expanding our consciousness and, in many cases, leaving aside the beliefs of destruction. It means that we understand the roles we play, their scope, and how we build a sustainable world, parting from families to industries and institutions.

Many people frame this evolution in spiritual growth. I do believe it is, but I am not placing any religion belief above another when I talk about the spiritual belief. I am looking for an understanding about that every belief is essential in our evolutionary process. As a species, coming to respect human existence is vital to advance as human beings in society.

I see spiritual growth as a process of understanding each human being as a person, understanding emotions, sensations, and perceptions that we have, including our language. I see spiritual growth as a means to transform all destructive emotions, feelings, and perceptions through understanding our human existence. Those who believe in post-life experiences or even those who do not, will lead us to a more peaceful, harmonious coexistence of greater welfare and prosperity.

2.1 EVOLUTIONARY GROWTH THROUGH SPIRITUAL GROWTH OR THE UNDERSTANDING OF EVOLUTION

Much is said about development indicators, but it is complicated to reduce poverty if we do not change adults' behavior: Those who treasure and those who have nothing and work for treasuring. The consciousness we accomplish as adults can lead us to achieve a more friendly behavior towards the planet, greater sustainability, and a capacity to generate life from prosperity and well-being.

There is no way to generate development if we cannot understand that life itself is essential. We can translate evolutionary growth as spiritual growth, without confusing it with religion, as we know that human being is also composed of spirit and consciousness. When many individuals grow spiritually, they allow themselves to build a more harmonic planet. These individuals lead us to understand that part of evolution is to know how to manage the resources we have on Earth at the service of all those who inhabit it.

Throughout human history, much of life experiences have been wars. The need to conquer, take away, treasure, and possess, have led us to believe that these are almost natural expressions of humankind. But these expressions are derived from the most primitive thing we have: our instinct. Suppose we do not migrate from this belief. In that case, we will not evolve to generate less instinctive and more conscious behaviors.

Every time instinct wins over the reason of being and respect for human existence as a species, we destroy entire nations, causing irreparable pain and suffering, generation after generation. I believe that wars have made it clear that this is not the way forward as a species. Each war leaves so much destruction, leading to repetition over and over again, to the point where, as a species, we are always condemned to repeat the same story.

And suppose we add to this historical moment the disdain for the elderly and all they have learned in their human existence. In that case, we can see that we are continuing down the path of destruction again and again.

A bomb exploding anywhere in the world affects the whole planet and, there is no way to migrate to another planet yet. The sense of destruction brings along the destruction of ourselves.

The whole planet is one house with many rooms. If the house is destroyed, all of its inhabitants will be affected. Physically we can have differences, substantial and evident. Still, no human has finished his life carrying away all he has treasured. *NOTHING PHYSICAL THAT HAS EXISTED ON EARTH* has been able to be transported by someone who ceases to exist.

And although it is not clear what comes after what we call death and, although some argue that there are proven experiences beyond death, and others state that there are not, the ONLY certainty is that we all have a physical experience on this planet. This planet is limited in resources, resources that help us maintain our life experience as we know it.

If we look at planet Earth from anywhere in the universe, we can see that naturally, there are no divisions.

The only divisions that exist are those invented by humankind. All living beings on the planet have a destiny: to be born, to grow, in many cases to reproduce and then die. In this sense, the wealthiest being on the Earth dies as the poorest child dies. All of us are going to leave the planet at some time. Neither the good nor the bad have been able to stay more than their existence allows. So, the variable we have in common as a whole is physical experience, which is finite.

Based on the experience we have as humans we can change our actions for future generations. Suppose we expand consciousness and act less in an instinctive, reactive way or what I call the Ego way (that irrational way of wanting always to be right), which operates from that system of beliefs. In that case, we will give them a different heritage. This system lacks the expressions of the being, which leads us to a greater understanding of the human species.

2.2 The Importance of Personal and Spiritual Growth for Society

We cannot advance towards a model of sustained growth when individual interests take precedence over collective interests. Immersed in a society that supports only physical and material development because of the discontent generated by inequality, violence, corruption and an excess of hierarchies and domains. Additionally, the ignorance or lack of interest of people and nations allow the election of people who claim to represent their interests, but after a while, end up subjecting their constituents to inferior conditions to those they live as leaders.

Any kind of dictatorship or political condition of government that leads to the benefit of a few is full of Ego, of power that leads peoples and nations to be in constant wars, disputes and disagreements, without representing in the least the needs of people. A few people's interest is transferred, encouraging and generating hatred between people, to cause division that does not allow to advance towards agreements that may lead to a real prosperity and welfare of society.

Hatreds between the social classes, different political parties, religions, races of the human species, and hierarchies within the productive sector are instigated by a few who want to remain at the top of the power pyramid, leading many individuals to become infected by hatred and thus fight uselessly. At the same time, the leaders enjoy great luxuries and benefits, regardless of the suffering, pain, poverty and misery in which people live.

As a species, we have been able to destroy entire cities, create diseases and subject human existence to the destruction of ourselves and even the planet. In exchange for what? For more wars and more hatred without moving towards a new chapter in our human species' history. We are responsible for the destruction. As a fact, we must explore new alternatives that respect humanity's existence in every sense of the word. Regardless of race, place of birth, beliefs, and the most valuable thing we have of this experience: life itself.

In reviewing the history of humanity, we take a look at the number of wars and confrontations that have the objective of domination: to own land, money, power. We even go through thinking that a human being is an object of possession. We have belittled human existence in every possible way. Be it women, children, or in the elderly, in people with different sexual preferences, in other religious beliefs, or simply because the mind dictates that "it" is less than each of "us". Other people's value judgments are loaded with prejudice, fear, pain, suffering, envy, superiority complexes, and greed. This happens to the point of destroying the other just because he gets in the way.

The "million-dollar" question is: How can we change the reality of human existence? After many years of study, my proposal is: Through personal growth based on spiritual growth, life and human existence are dignified. For a single moment, let us look at the fact that nations, companies in different productive sectors, government entities, schools ..., are made up or conformed by people. People who mark the path of humanity; and, if the mind of these people is the most significant expression of their Ego, the history of human existence will remain the same: wars, destruction, power, money, greed, violence.

Now, the goal of human existence must be different from satisfying physical needs, giving away power, goods, land, and, as I already expressed, even people. Changing the course and finding the real goal is done from a more holistic and spiritual approach. Only if the minds that lead the world bend their great Ego and understand and accept that we are all equal in this physical experience, despite the physical differences of races that over time have become mixed, to the point of understanding that we are one species. We are so similar that we all are born and all of us will die.

Simply stated: no one has ever been spared death and is here to tell that they got rid of it or that they took all their belongings and power for a post-physical and earthly experience.

2.3 Ego and Being

It is imperative to stop obeying Egos that lead us to destruction. It is necessary to take a different path, in which wielding or shooting weapons is not the solution. The solution is to raise the level of consciousness of as many people as we can. From that optimal level, we will allow ourselves to live together without feeling the need to conquer lands, order, dominate, and enslave.

All the expressions that come from our instinct and beliefs make us correspond to actions and situations full of hatred, pain, suffering, anguish, and fear. It is the very expression of our inability to evolve since we place the needs of the Ego in the first place, then expressed in excesses of all kinds.

The way to stop this absurd race of materialism is to focus on the process of spiritual and personal growth, healing our soul, which has been contaminated throughout life by painful experiences we were unable to handle.

These memories lead people to hold so many grudges and hatreds that at the end of life, revenge hatred, and the need to dominate others, will repeat the destructive cycle in which humans have lived forever.

Some people fight to own more land, more money, to own entire countries that, because of their ignorance of the spiritual world, they feel that should be given to them. Others, because they treasure and seek wealth, are capable of killing, eliminating, or removing from the path anyone who gets in the way of their plans to accumulate more material things. It is the decision of: I do want it, and I must do anything to have it, even if I end up hurting millions of people, families, children with my doing and subduing the whole planet for an apparent wealth that is not such, and letting our enormous Ego guide us.

For others, the stakes are to produce without measure, without care, and regardless of the environment's damage. Treasuring money and power are the watchword. They feel the urgent need to fill their pockets, disregarding the future of the resources that belong to humanity. Because of the Ego, which induces the need to own and be powerful, we have condemned several species to death and extinction due to the inexistent limits that could force us to take care of our planet, which in the end, is our common home, the home of all of living beings who inhabit it. We are all owners of the same misfortune that we have forged.

The Ego's power is so great that it inhabits people of all countries and nations. It does not exclude people from governments or companies; it can be both in public and private entities. It is the owner of everything and leads humankind to unconsciousness, to satisfy needs that do not exist in many cases and are only the anxiety of living like kings with all kinds of luxuries, no matter what.

Now, these people's "Being" seems to have disappeared between childhood and adulthood, with no possible return. They lead entire nations to condemn the new generations because infants absorb this behavior at a very early age. The reactivity of the Ego, the need of being right, and the unjustified capacity of destruction, just because someone wants it so.
As a species, we have fought for resources that any mind with power assumes should belong to him or her, regardless of human existence and the destruction of the planet.

The Ego has led humanity to such a state of apathy that that not the slightest compassion is shown for the pain of so many people in need. It is as if they did not exist. It is as if some had the right to possess everything without any measure. It is easy to see how the human species manifests the severity and capacity to self-destruct its own world, not noticing that we can be part of something else.

The loneliness to which the great egos are condemned is everything. Nothing satisfies their desire to have and own, to do my will, to command, to accumulate. And since their need is unstoppable, the destruction itself is unbeatable. It is so difficult that in this loneliness, emptiness of soul and heart, we reach the reason for the human species' existence to prevail. The Ego blinds people who believe themselves immortal, superior, gods. It even seems that their "belief" is that they come from another world just to command.

Greed and the inability to value the other one equally in our species condemn us to repeat wars and destruction over and over again. We see entire nations threatening to destroy a part of the planet. I still wonder: Do they already have a place to go? Is life on the earth so irrelevant for them so to have the capacity and the desire to destroy everything if people don't listen and obey them?

It is as if we are canceling out the possibility of considering others. That Ego that leads us to feel superior is apparent as it ignores that we all have a finite physical life experience and that we are all, without exception, going to die. And in the graveyard, only parts of our physical body will remain, but there is no more than that. Many will be remembered in a certain way. Still, we only have the possibility that some will know of our existence at the end of times, and others will never know that we became part of the planet.

Suppose we can get each of us to understand our own behaviors, where they come from, what we feel and what we think. In that circumstance, we will be able to create a different correspondence. We will allow this behavior to be changed into something more harmonious for everyone. It is worrying to find out that from the unconsciousness present in some of us who inhabit the planet, everything we create is destruction that will become an endless cycle.

The Ego feeds inequality, hatred, the inability to move on from the past, centuries of violence with a desire for revenge for millions of years, leaving in its way a species anchored to endless suffering and without any capacity to manage emotions or sensations. With a perception of superiority in some people and of inferiority in others, fact that submits and places the human species to be the one that finally will end this planet. The only apparent benefit will be for the powerful ones, the owners of the money, the dominators This power is the one that marks the way for a significant number of "*ignorant*" people to follow them, only based on the belief that those powerful ones will do something for humanity. In the end, we see that the powerful guys do nothing for the planet or for anyone, only because they have the comforts they want, and they need other believers, to stay in power.

When I refer to "*ignorant*", I mean people who do not manage, from their awakening of consciousness, to understand the correspondences we cause by performing one action or another.

2.4 Correspondences

We may or may not give a meaning to everything that shows up in our life. From Gerardo Schmelding's point of view, we can understand that life is a chain of correspondences depending on the evolution level that a person is experiencing at certain moment.

In this sense, I can affirm that everything that happens passes through correspondence. In my book "*The Power of Being*", I explain that each human being becomes corresponding with a certain level of learning and that each person is the architect of his life. It is assumed that everything has a meaning and that things happen because you or me wanted it, generated it, or allowed it. It does not matter if one knows or not about the Laws of the Universe. If, as an individual, I react to violence with more violence, I will be corresponding with seven times more of everything I emit and do. It is a complex thought that leads us to think that everything that is broadcasted, multiplies on the planet. And worse, if so, no body longer controls this multiplication as if I could handle not emitting violence, that is, the initial act.

However, to decide not to emit violence, I must have the capacity to control my emotions and thoughts. It is in the mental level, where everything that will end up being an action, is gestated.

In other words, it is in the mental level where I will generate or manifest what can be transformed into an action. Before being an action, it is a thought. Before being a thought, it is a stimulus that the body receives, and this stimulus enters through our senses. By entering the body, the brain receives and carries out a physical and a chemical response. A cognitive process is then translated into thoughts, which will end up being an action when related to history or what is recorded in an individual's long-term memory.

If I need to change the action, it is essential to work on the thought. The focus of attention is not taken to the cognitive process and generates a violent reaction. For this to happen, it is necessary to change the focus of attention and place that attention on other stimuli so that the result is harmonious. When the action is executed, no chain of instincts will lead us to react violently or alter the system of beliefs, feeling the need of the Ego to create a reaction that alters the harmony.

Given that altering harmony builds a violent response, in most cases, we seek to achieve a reaction with a higher level of consciousness to correspond with the environment and the interior. In this way, we are more in tune with the spiritual development than with the basic needs of the Ego.

The correspondence has led us to be anchored to the instinct as humanity, reacting again and again. Raising the consciousness level allows us to create a way of life following harmony and with the spiritual response, which is slower, wiser, calmer, and generates harmony.

If we act from consciousness, a more harmonious form of correspondence will be created, which is more respectful of every species. With a higher level of consciousness, as a human species, we will correspond with:

- Fewer natural and human disasters.
- Fewer alterations to ecosystems.
- Tremendous respect for life.

- Outstanding care.
- Greater capacity for cooperation.
- Learning respect for different species.

This will all lead us to grow and develop our social and environmental consciousness and, as a result, correspond with the planet that can be more sustainable.

2.5 EVOLUTION

Evolution occurs when a system that is more coherent with the needs of humanity and in accordance with the planet is created, leading us to produce the right quantities, to respect the environment, to be responsible with families, to build fair compensation agreements and to be able, from solidarity and compassion, to support accountable supply and demand.

A higher level of awareness is indispensable to build a new Earth where all actors and economic agents' role are valued. We will then find gender equality, supporting children's socio-emotional and cognitive development, building networks of support to contribute to health because mental and physical health are the center of a healthy society.

Evolution leads us to be a species that can live on the planet in a state of harmony, where waste is less, where the capacity to absorb the supply is by the needs of the regions and not those of the Ego of those who produce excessively. Evolution implies respect for all. It is necessary to reconsider, as the ancient tribes did, the elders' importance and the wisdom of the oldest people. We must rescue all those who have lost the ability to be functional in society due to the lack of resources, forgetfulness and even neglect.

Although youth have an impact and is full of energy, evolution allows us to value previous experiences to continue working in a more productive cycle that generates greater well-being.

The concept of how revitalizing can be for a society the drive and tenacity of its young people, their desire to do things in different ways, their impetus and desire to advance the frontier of knowledge can be valuable "*IN FAIR MEASUREMENT*". Then if we do chain the idea that the evolution of conscience CAN bring to youth the possibility of integrating the knowledge and the wisdom of the previous generations in PRO of the common well-being.

To build societies from cooperation allows the balancing of the levels of inequality that only lead to resentments and the incapacities to advance as a social planet. The evolution is directed to the fact that we are one species, and everything is interconnected.

3. NEW EARTH

3.1. WOMEN AS AN EVOLUTIONARY FACTOR

The role of women is fundamental to reach evolution because of their unique characteristics. When I look at women, I do not see them as an equal entity by itself and by its fair value because equality on the planet does not work. If we could talk about equality, we should all be totally equal and, in the end, we are not. Therefore, it is mandatory to appreciate women from a point of impartiality and love.

Women are the center of evolution and prosperity. Although women's role has changed over the years, there are still countries in which women do not have freedom, do not vote, or exercise clear leadership. But, day by day, the reality changes, and equality between genders becomes a prevailing necessity. The salaries must be assigned by the capabilities and not by gender. There are initiatives in Latin American countries to equalize the gender wage gap; however, there is still a long way to go.

To achieve real parity, we must emphasize that on a new level of awareness, family must be the center of attention and of development of society, so to earn respect for life and for each of its members' personal and professional growth. If we quote Maslow, we can recognize that in the pyramid of needs, every human being has: physiological needs (breathing, feeding, rest, sex) that are related to self-care; security needs (physical, employment, obtaining resources, moral, family health and even prosperity), filiation needs (friendship, affection, sexual intimacy), recognition needs (self-recognition, confidence, respect, success) and self-relationship (morality, creativity, spontaneity, lack of prejudice, acceptance).

In a new level of consciousness, all individuals in the planet must satisfy their needs without tints of exclusion.

One step to achieve this is to promote equal treatment and opportunities between genders, even more so in the working environment. And not only equality, but also justness. It is crucial to understand equality as the ability to provide society with similar conditions to meet the planet's needs.

Disregarding the importance of everything that happens to women within the family due to labor and social differences, and how this will greatly affect children who grow up with affective limitations, because they are not being able to relate with a family where love and parents time prevails, from a state of understanding the development stage of each individual.

That is to say, to recognize that everything that is done for women, men, children and family, affects positively the mental health, the stability and even the spiritual and individual development of each member of the family.

Equality seeks that women are paid the same as men; that when they need leave, pre-established solutions exist to obtain it without difficulties or objections. Equality is an agreement to work without referring to gender. In case of needing differentiation, it should be done by competencies, knowledge, and skills evaluated by applying tests. Although the male brain conditions may generate excellent abilities in certain aspects or fields, this does not exclude that the female's brain may also be very good at the man's same ability.

Like men, women have time to be productive and, at that same time, are also fertile. Society must respect women's right to be mothers. It respects her by being a cooperative society, where we all collaborate. Thus, if a woman decides to be a mother, the same society of cooperation supports and helps her. Those new children who arrive to this planet can count on mother's time and may be full of love.

For this reason, I believe that companies should allow not only breastfeeding time. A more extended period should be granted instead, by generating schemes of teleworking or flexible hiring systems so that women can take care of their children for at least six months or more.

Breastfeeding should be a fundamental right, from that point of love.

According to the World Health Organization (WHO) and the United Nations Children's Fund (UNICEF), breastfeeding is essential during the first six months of a baby's life because it benefits both children and their mothers.

In the first six months of life, an exclusive mother milk diet provides all the energy and nutrients that a child need. It ensures that the baby's growth, health, and development are optimal. It protects children from infectious and chronic diseases. Breast milk contains antibodies that defend them from deadly diseases common in infants, such as diarrhea and pneumonia. Promotes sensory and cognitive development; the baby develops robust, healthy, and intelligent.

Breastfeeding is not only limited to the first six months of life; it should be maintained, not exclusively, until after the baby is two years old.

In the long term, breast milk promotes good health throughout life. Breastfed children are less likely to suffer from obesity, overweight, and diabetes in their adult life; they also have better results in intelligence tests and are associated with significant educational achievements and improving babies' motor development.

On an emotional level, breastfeeding generates a special bond between mother and child. The longer the breastfeeding period, the greater the maternal response capacity and the greater the emotional security that the bond provides.

On the mother's side, breastfeeding reduces the risk of postpartum depression and anemia, helps her lose weight, reduces the risk of breast and ovarian cancer and reduces the risk of osteoporosis after menopause.

Also, it is essential to consider the time in which a woman is raising children. Society itself should think of alternatives so that children can enjoy their mothers at least in the first five years, which are of vital importance for their later development, taking into account mothers' non-stigmatization when they are housewives.

I will tell you a personal anecdote: When I wanted to return to the formal working world after my son's birth, in a job interview, the person who received me said: "Ahhh... You have not done anything during these three years that you have been raising your child".

I ask myself: have you done nothing by assuring security and love to a child so that he or she can be an excellent human being in the future? My idea is to reach a point of evolution where those mothers who dedicate time to their homes are justly valued. Thanks to that attention and dedication, better citizens are developed.

Homeschooling or Home education, is a training style in which parents decide to educate their children without educational institutions' intervention. With this alternative, the children learn creatively and differently from the traditional way. It promotes the child's autonomy and his learning through experience and curiosity. It makes them responsible for the schedule and education; they grow and strengthen their independence and learn to love training and doing new things. Creating social relationships is through extracurricular activities, to which children dedicate more time, such as sports, music and art.

Education thus focuses on enhancing the student's qualities and skills. Parents influence their children by spending more quality time together. Parents are directly involved with the educational model by choosing the one that best suits their preferences.

Capitalism has led us to that position of a foreman, to that "macho" society, in which women can do little or nothing at all. There is simply a boss and a secretary, without realizing that the man could also be a secretary. It was because of this lack of equality that feminism was born. When we talk about equality, we talk about eradicating "machismo" without extremism, without falling into radical positions. Women can stay at home without being stigmatized when they want to enter the labor market again.

When we talk about the economy and evolution, both genders are necessary. Any expression or sexual condition must be respected to reach the evolution where there will be total respect of the Being. The Self is the active expression of a living entity experiencing something on Earth, so we should consider any individual, regardless of whether we understand their position.

The economy of evolution refers to achieving an understanding from capitalism point of view, that women deserve the same respect as any other individual, and we should work in justness, and give them that fundamental role that has been denied in many places around the world.

By equality, I mean establishing that she can have the time for childcare and also, to start looking for ways to make women and men be paid equally.

According to the International Labor Organization's (ILO) Global Wage Report 2018/2019, women worldwide continue to be paid approximately 20% less than men for comparable work. This report covers 70 countries and nearly 80% of the world's wage earners.

The report reveals that gender wage gaps are highest at the top end of the wage scale in high-income countries. In contrast, in low- or middle-income countries, the difference is most remarkable among the lowest-paid workers.

One of the reasons for this gender pay gap is maternity. Women with children generally earn lower wages than women without children. Reduced working hours, career breaks, and stereotyped decisions about promotions in the company are some of the factors that impact this situation. Even before women experience motherhood, inequality in payment already exists.

In 2015, the UN approved the "Sustainable Development Goals". That is, it approved 17 goals to be achieved to transform the world by 2030. One of these goals is precisely Gender Equality, which seeks to achieve gender fairness and empower all women and girls by eliminating violence, discrimination and harmful practices such as child marriage. Additionally, ensuring women's full and effective participation in political, economic, and public scopes and allowing that equal rights for men and women's financial resources are taken into account.

Another Sustainable Development Objective that talks about gender equality concerning work is: "Decent work and economic growth." This seeks, among all its goals, equal pay for work of equal valuation since, according to the UN: "the gender wage gap worldwide stands at 23% and, if no action is taken, it will take another 68 years to achieve pay equity. The rate of participation of women in the workforce is 63%, while that of men is 94%".

When we talk about the economy and evolution, we are talking about re-establishing the UN's same fundamental rights for all. Among these we can state: the right to have a job freely chosen, with equitable and satisfactory conditions, the right for receiving equal payment for equal work without discrimination, the right to fair and adequate remuneration that ensures a dignified existence for him or her and their family, and the right to paid rest. Motherhood and childhood have the right to special care and assistance, the right to education, and the right to have a family.

On the other hand, women in society are a pillar for the activation of any economy. They are the ones who most encourage consumption. Some studies show that women are the ones who generate more demand and consumption, even if men pay for it. The woman is the one in society who usually craves for things, and this is common to many cultures. That is why it is imperative to understand that women also activate any economic reactivation or economic growth.

For example, in Western society, women are the motor of production, the vital agent of the capitalist system. They are active consumers and responsible for purchasing goods, even in more than 80% of families. They are agents of change and poverty reduction. Investing in women's education promotes collaborative, social, economic, and spiritual development.

Moreover, moving a population away from poverty has an impact on the entire planet. Women are a fundamental pillar for the growth of a more conscious, more capable, more loving society. They lead us to heal the deepest wounds and are, from a holistic point of view, those who can guide society with immense love and understanding.

The new capitalist systems need the balance of feminine energy to build self-caring societies, understanding ones, with capacities, respect, and kindness. We need to balance the energies, go from just doing and owning to creating and sustaining. Being with sustainable behavioral and caring for the planet and all its inhabitants is a must. To achieve harmony and a higher level of consciousness in society, there must be women guiding the way, without falling into excesses and exclusions.

We must highlight women's roles throughout history to understand that genders are equally important. Both male and female energy is a single expression of the Self. Both points are vital and must be in balance. To evolve and grow, it is necessary to transcend thoughts such as "I don't need a man to be a mother" or "we don't need women in the business world."

From the Family Constellations scope, we can see, in the most accurate way that we all have a place in the family, and our own space to respect. And though there are family absences, it is vital to avoid generating resentments and understanding that both parents are necessary for its evolution.

As women, to have the capacity to recognize men's roles and men also, to recognize the fundamental role of women in society. And from the recognition and acceptance, to assume respect for each one's position. In the situation where someone is missing, respect their place as a parent, ensuring spaces of love for them; that is, conditions of understanding for the other's existence.

Focusing on family and giving support as a society to reduce the levels of violence through the development of awareness in families. This will allow infants' growth in spaces full of love, mental health, physical health and therefore improvement in society and the sustainability of the human species.

Domestic violence occurs in all social strata, from the poorest to the wealthiest. It limits the capacity of infants' cognitive, emotional, social and even spiritual development, generating more resentment, hatred, and destruction to society.

We can say with total certainty: the human species has not had a year of life in complete peace on planet Earth. Reviewing history leads us to understand that our development at the level of consciousness has gone through the first levels: slavery, war, ignorance, toxic systems, wars for power, conflicts between beliefs and religions, imposition of socialist and capitalist systems, wars for possessions and land. It is time to move to economic systems centered on a higher level of consciousness. A system that allows the family to be the center invites companies to respect the time children need with their parents to grow, to take care of their health from the beginning and to understand the cycle of life. This translates into actions such as valuing the first stage of life and generating systems that encourage breastfeeding in the first year.

Another appropriate business decision is to support the family unity at the time of birth; father and mother should have permits so to grow in family and society and allow teleworking in many moments. Design spaces to be teams and collaborators. Parents can be attentive to their children's school development. There should be no answers like "I don't care about school meetings. You have to be on time."

We are talking about being equitable with the families so that at least one of the two parents can help to look after the children without being maltreated. In the cases in which women cannot stay away from work, there could be the free choice by which a man can also cover these aspects of childcare.

By highlighting the fundamental role of women, we are not saying that men cannot do it. We are saying that at least one of the parents and society should take care of the children.

By understanding that children's education and accompaniment reduce violence and social diseases (drug trafficking, illegal activities, crimes, etc.), States could dedicate more resources to education than to control violence. The economies that have bet on education, such as Japan, China, and Finland, have recognized childhood as an important stage for action and have grown economically faster than those still betting on war.

3.2. CHILDHOOD IS A TREASURE.
Child development and their cognitive development go hand in hand with children's experiences in their environment. Breastfeeding, as I said earlier, is vital to prevent the spread of disease. Still, more importantly, it promotes the mental health of both mother and child. The bond created between them and the ability to recognize each other from the moment of birth allows the improvement of human species' performance and development.

Then again, the time to act is now. We must respect, support and encourage the importance of family in the development of infants. Children who manage to grow up in healthier mental environments build strong self-esteem, thus developing many more human and physical competencies to construct a more prosperous future. I speak of prosperity from the vision of balance in all aspects of life as a whole, not from the monetary aspect.

The way children learn is from observing adult behavior. If we adults do not understand the importance of our children's development actions, we will continue to deform the future. This will be starting from the ignorance that has led human existence to remain in wars and not knowing a sustainable and sustainable growth.

The importance of education in the family and social ambit explains the rapid and successful economic progress that China has made in the past three decades, to the point of being recognized as having one of the best educational systems in the world.

The educational system is a comprehensive system in which teachers, parents and educational authorities ensure students' development and success. Thus, education is free and compulsory in primary school, consisting of six years, and in junior high school, which consists of three years. The school environment is developed, focusing on competitiveness, dedication and extreme pressure, where the only thing that matters is quality and being the best.

China has understood that the basis of development and progress is education and, as a result, annually invests billions of dollars in its students. Likewise, the exigency is very high. Students must pass an exam to enter the second cycle of secondary school. Then, to enter university, they must take the most severe national exam, with the greatest pressure and competition, worldwide speaking. They prepare their entire school life for that moment in which their professional life, social status and future are at stake.

They have 2145 higher education institutions and 12 million students who understand that the world's economy depends on what they do with what they know. They desire to prepare themselves and one day give back to their country what it has done for them. They grow up with the idea of giving back to society everything the country has given them.

Finland is another example. It is a country where politicians, school principals, teachers and universities have understood that their only and most important resource is education. Therefore, this resource must have all the attention; children and young people are the country's brain. All the decisions are oriented to fulfill the same objective: to offer children an education model that makes them competitive in the international market. This understanding has created an education system so strong and amazing that it has the highest quality standards worldwide and is number one in almost all international qualification systems. This system is based on the "Integrated School" on the teachers' confidence and professionalism.

The Integrated School is aimed at all young people, giving them the same opportunities, and the same curriculum without economic, social or cultural distinction. Education is based on the principles of equality and fairness.

The government of any country establishes the basic curriculum. The schools have the freedom to adapt and carry out their own curriculum and make their own decisions having as main tools innovation and entrepreneurship, which must be in each subject and in each class program just like art. Each class has more time and fewer classes per day. This allows students to have more time to carry out their projects and prioritize academic tasks.

In Finland, students learn to use knowledge, which is more important than learning how to repeat; they learn to find their answers.

Trust plays a significant role as it is from this value that the entire Finnish educational system is built. The minister hopes that municipalities will adopt and adapt the national curriculum according to their needs. Municipalities trust that local schools and teachers will do the right thing. Teachers trust that students use the right time for their assignments, the internet and other technologies. Parents rely on the education system to shape their children for a rich, fulfilling and productive life in the new global knowledge economy.

Trust is so high that they have no one to control or audit whether schools and teachers are doing their jobs. Even students do not have many evaluations or assignments, fact which allows each student to find the best way to learn. Classes are based on 60% students and 40% teachers, allowing teachers to focus on the young people who need it most.

Finally, the professionalism of teachers is of high quality. To become a teacher, people must have a master's degree, which meets the high standards for admission to schools. Only students with the highest level of preparation and performance become teachers. The teaching practices take place directly in the classroom where they learn from other teachers that may act as tutors, prepare their classes and receive feedback at the end of the day. In other words, they are students - teachers who prepare themselves to captivate all their students.

Teachers are knowledge builders, team workers who see the classroom as a laboratory for continuous innovation and seek to ensure that all students have access to the best and highest education levels. They are in charge of facilitating the collective work of the students. That is why Finnish society has such confidence in them.

Being a teacher is a highly demanded profession in Finland, to which they dedicate themselves from their youth until their retirement age. They have an excellent reputation and are a solid union.

This indicates an admiration for knowledge. Knowledge and respect lead a society to build high confidence, to tend to a sustainable and supportable development, creating synergy for the future, so that the new generations have prosperity. It has a permanent commitment for development and to the ability to transmit knowledge at this level of wisdom. In this way, all citizens of their country have a quality of life desirable by everyone on the planet.

Education is the essential tool for building a sustainable planet. An education based on respect that may lead to a high level of awareness will allow them to materialize prosperity in the present moment and generate a promising future for all.

3.2.1. THE FUTURE IS ADULTS' RESPONSIBILITY

As stated before, the family is the nucleus of all society and the clearest way to transcend the knowledge that we will carry on planet Earth. Companies must support children's development, understanding the importance of the family. We must promote being family-conscious and family-responsible companies so that we can be aligned with evolutionary development.

The neglect and mistreatment of families fractures the most important unit of society. Companies are made up of people, and all the people who work in them have families. Families that it is imperative to heal so to make them the best place for our children.

Suppose we change the current bet, where the companies consume all the productive time of the families' members to produce. They may ignore the damage that is done to children by the abandonment of their parents. Parents are thus incapable, in terms of time, to face the responsibilities of raising their children with their actual physical presence as parents. If they could have more time with their children, then, raising would not be a job for another person.. In that case, we could build a more sustainable planet.

Children do not only need quality time; they also need quantity of time. And the business world must be co-responsible for children, making the sustainability of families the core of their development.

This commitment must not remain on paper or in a plan of objectives at a global level. It is necessary to move from the desire to protect children and families to concrete facts. Businesses and entrepreneurs are responsible for tirelessly pursuing only material goals such as the accumulation of money and power in exchange for the destruction of many millions of families.

The system must understand that business plans must include the well-being of the people who work in the companies. Let us remember that companies are made up of people, and as we mentioned before, each individual is part of a family.

Establishing that managers have skills to manage a company, assuming the idea that it is more important to be in the company even though they could be neglecting their family, is common to do to achieve an economic result. However, everything is relevant: both the profit of companies as production units that allow managing the wealth and even prosperity of those who work there and the welfare and the importance of meeting the needs of families.

Now, we think that only children from poor families are abandoned to get money for their sustenance. Well, they are just as unfortunate as children from families with great purchasing power whose parents pay for their upbringing. Their parents cannot be present for the same reason: because they are getting money. At the end of the story, all children are going to have big emotional deficiencies that will lead them not to have an inner and outer balance.

It is vital to recognize that families need time, care, and support from all the agents who are involved. We have gone through centuries of wars, abrupt separations and fears created by dysfunctions in families that range from violence to abandonment, year after year. And this reality goes on without being able to write a different story.

The family is the most essential and fundamental nucleus. Achieving a balance between family and work life is the challenge we must overcome, leaving aside the belief that money is the center of everything.

To cooperate within a community to achieve prosperity and development will be possible only if we are able to put the Being before the Ego and create environments of mutual support to fulfill the dreams of the companies and the balanced development of the families. By doing so, we will have a generation of children (perhaps utopic) with mental, emotional, and material balance.

3.3 Prosperity and Old Age

There are certain cultures in which young people take care of the elderly and learn from them. There are certain places in the world where the senior people are allowed to work to form companies, such as Silicon Valley. There are places where the elder people teach young people, but on the other hand, there are many places on the planet where the elderly are despised and forgotten.

Therefore, the importance of a pension at the end of life and a dignified old age lies in the adult and elderly population's care. We must change the way of valuing them.

In the ancestral cultures, there is a great respect for the older population; they are the ones who possess the wisdom for what they have lived. They are living proof of history, that if we repeat it, we return to wars, destruction, unconsciousness, inability to respect others and our own planet. It is imperative to look back at the wellness systems for the elderly in order to transform the contempt for old age into a bank of enriching experiences for personal growth and thus reach higher levels of awareness.

One of the most innovative projects regarding old age is or "Home that fits". This project is developed in Finland and consists of young people under 25 years old being allowed to live in elderly homes for one year at a low cost. They have a sole condition that they dedicate three to five hours a week to their elderly neighbors.

This project aims to help young people find reasonably priced housing (Helsinki is one of the most expensive cities in the world to rent a place) and also to provide social benefits to the elderly at their homes. Older people have a lot to give and share; they have much experience too, but they do not have an active social life at that point. Hence, interaction with young people makes it easier for them to share their wisdom and to be seen.

According to a U.S. National Academy of Sciences report in 2012, social isolation and loneliness in the elderly are associated with increased mortality. According to this, in the Netherlands, a program was implemented: University students can live in nursing homes for free. The only condition is that they be "good neighbors" for at least 30 hours a month to take part in avoiding the adverse effects of aging in elder people.

When we speak of evolution, we speak of being able to bring the elder ones to the possibility of being at peace, of transmitting, of teaching, of generating and giving love, of taking advantage of their expertise, of creating places where their knowledge and wisdom are valued, of restoring their right to expression, of treating them with fairness and respect because we are simply missing out on great wisdom. We must return to the ancestral way where the older adult represents wisdom. Today, elder people are despised and felt as a burden; they are just there to die. We must change that way of seeing them.

In China, in families, parents and grandparents live together, with the great advantage that the grandparents are always looking after their grandchildren's education. This makes the families a little more united. In addition, in ancient cultures such as Japan and China, the respect they have for their elders is evident.

Although my ideal model is not to live with grandparents, it would be essential to rescue the respect that is held for the elderly. On this side of the world, respect has been so much lost that even in places like Silicon Valley, the elderly are taken to institutions that are exclusive for them. As children, they are taken care for by a nanny and, as adults, they end up being cared for by another nanny. In my concept, that kind of world is not right. Love, wisdom, knowledge is "wasted" by not giving them the attention and care that our grandparents deserve, by not making them feel loved.

My model of the economy of evolution understands the value of the elderly, giving them and ensuring them at least a minimum pension, a minimum of sustainability, everything necessary with respect to health, and allowing them to be productive if they want to. According to studies, when they retire, many die from inactivity and depression because there comes a time when this causes the person to lose his self-esteem, lose his cognitive skills to end up with no life at all.

In economic systems, older adults are generally not expected to last long because they are a financial burden. For this reason, we should think about alternatives to maintain and use their wisdom and productivity (if possible), and we should reconsider and understand that they are still part of the economic, cultural, and historical knowledge and that their experience can generate greater maturity in young people and children, as well as in the families themselves.

Governments know that the economic costs of caring for the elderly are high. That is why, in Finland, they solve the problem by keeping the elderly physically active and socially involved. The government ensures that they do not have to live in poverty; they provide them with easily accessible and discounted facilities, making it easier for them to enjoy public transportation, an exercise in swimming pools, gyms, and parks, and visit museums, libraries, and theaters. They enjoy social events, scheduled trips and are increasingly part of volunteer programs that support other seniors and school-age children. Housing has also been adjusted to the needs of the elderly, such as collaborative, innovative, and self-sufficient housing.

3.4 CHANGES IN THE ECONOMIC APPROACH

I propose to create what I call the Responsible Economy, fair Capitalism, without dictatorships, with Balance and Respect as the center of everything. Respect for each individual and their growth, respect and appreciation for children, being the present the most important time. Respect for the care of our mother earth. And every part of this proposal, from recognizing that the most critical dimension to achieve a higher level of economic growth in societies is to understand that society is composed of individuals.

Each one of them can generate an economic dimension that translates into the ability to monetize the learned skills, knowledge without the fears and defects that have been appropriated throughout life.

Individual = Economic dimension

= monetizing capacity

(abilities + knowledge − fears − defects)

This personal dimension has been given from the family bosom and the environment, and it begins from childhood. The acquired knowledge, the learned values, the learned behaviors of authority and affection, and the lived experiences that remain installed as each individual's structure, makes individuals to create reality that they wish.

This process can be conscious or unconscious and, to change or work on spiritual development and to reach a higher level of consciousness on a planetary level, that personal dimension becomes important. This leads us immediately to commit ourselves to work for a childhood without violent experiences, for having respect of all individuals, for families and their mental, emotional and economic health.

Economic dimension (personal dimension)

$= \Sigma$ *personal dimension of n individuals*

The personal dimension must focus on generating self-knowledge, valuing the inner and outer world, and having experiences that heal at a planetary level, all the wounds opened by the past. To recognize that the personal dimension takes us to a closer level to satisfy the basic needs, more from the true wealth: prosperity in love and understanding, not only the accumulation of goods and properties.

Economical Dimension (Personal Dimension)

$$= \Sigma \text{ personal dimension of } n \text{ individuals}$$

Personal dimension =

(Learned values:

$\pm$ *Affecction and authority behaviors*

$\pm$ *Life experience* $\pm$ *knowledge*

To work in the personal dimension is to heal the figures of authority and affection. It is to recognize, accept, and value the experiences of life to transmute suffering and do the necessary duels to reach inner peace from those experiences. It is to recognize that to manage a society from the Ego leads us to destruction. To allow that through the self-knowledge of the individuals at a planetary level, to heal relationships, to contribute to the balance from our inner work, we can recognize the purpose of human existence. This is the greatest challenge that leaders, companies, and society itself have.

The society based on Egos does not allow us to be a sustainable species in time. Its capacity of destruction is superior to the current construction capacity that society itself has. That is why it is vital to unite the economy and the spiritual growth in a single path.

Only if we allow ourselves to understand that individuals need to stop living from his Ego and agree on spiritual and personal growth, to build a society full of expressions of the Self, from the understanding, compassion, respect and appreciation of the other, we can create a conscious economy. Its wisdom will rely on the fact that, from the personal dimension, a greater level of conscience is achieved in each individual. Thus, we will reach an economy in which society is controlled by promoting responsible consumption, suitable production, land use with aims of planetary prosperity and not individual wealth.

The inability to avoid the massive destruction of environmental resources and stop the violence comes from our inability in managing the Ego. The Ego of the leaders is the one that evades being at service of their people. It leads the great multitudes to react from the beliefs; it delays consciousness's development a planetary level. It is increasingly important to be aware of the personal dimension so that we can achieve a different path and be a sustainable species.

Are we functioning as a society or are we leading to the same extinction? If, as a planet, we are not functioning, what should we do to change that? We have been at war for many, hundreds, thousands of years. Do we have a chance to stop being at war or will war continue to be a possibility for economic revival?

3.5 Leading from consciousness.

Starting from all the above and assuming the leaders' responsibility for the construction of a sustained and sustainable planet, changes are needed at all levels. Accepting the challenge for equality, respect and care, stop ignoring the balance of the Egos and the path to the destruction of the planet, of families, to the creation of violence that has remained throughout human existence.

We need each and every one of the leaders, people in business, rulers, to approach a higher level of consciousness, to stop putting their Ego first, and try to build a planet where respect for life, family, children, women, and old age, stop being plans on paper and become actions.

We must recognize that each one has the power in his hands. The change comes from understanding the inner world and giving place to personal and spiritual growth with management tools. Egos have ruled for millions of years. Although we have advanced in science and technology, it is time to move forward in being a harmonious human species, regardless of race, gender, age, or social class.

Leaders have a great responsibility in managing change, creating spaces for equality, respecting children and families, stopping along the way and planning the world from a higher level of consciousness, which seeks to end poverty, especially mental and spiritual poverty. They must build roads so that the economy is not the excuse to destroy us.

To think in a society where the planet does not need borders because we are not a danger for each other, promoting solidarity, collaboration and especially love as a state of understanding to evolve.

We are the product of all that we have not healed within ourselves, of resentments that are not left behind, of fears that lead us to attack, of the need to treasure without thinking of others. I propose to work for being a world where we help each other to be healthy, to change resentment for understanding, to support each other as a human species, to transform our thinking to build and create prosperity and wealth from that personal dimension.

Each one is responsible for its personal dimension, and each leader can start by raising its level of consciousness, working on its interiority, and understand its Ego, to transform its environment and thus transform our planet into a place where death and destruction are not daily news.

Let us seek that academies stop seeing soft skills as something intangible. They are as tangible as the destruction we have created. Let leadership schools and the school system build curricula to generate conscious citizens with skills that allow access to emotional intelligence to all people.

As mentioned, and studied by Goleman, make them discover the purpose of life not as a business plan but as a plan to create prosperity on a planetary level. Make companies and institutions validate equality for women on daily basis. Make us respect and value families as the central and vital nucleus of our development.

It is time to take responsibility for our spiritual, personal, and planetary growth.

BIBLIOGRAPHY

ABC. (7 de Octubre de 2013). *Harvard se rifa a los niños educados en casa.* Recuperado el 22 de Octubre de 2020, de ABC: https://www.abc.es/familia-padres-hijos/20131007/abci-homeschooling-educacion-familia-201309231231.html?ref=https:%2F%2Fwww.google.com%2F

Andrew Steptoe, A. S. (9 de Abril de 2013). *Social isolation, loneliness, and all-cause mortality in older men and women.* Recuperado el 27 de Octubre de 2020, de PNAS: https://www.pnas.org/content/110/15/5797.full

Aula Planeta. (5 de Febrero de 2018). *Homeschooling: educando en casa.* Recuperado el 21 de Octubre de 2020, de Aula Planeta: https://www.aulaplaneta.com/2018/02/05/en-familia/homeschooling-educando-casa/

Canal Once. (3 de Noviembre de 2014). *Documental - China, el gigante asiático. Educación, la clave del progreso.* Recuperado el 27 de Octubre de 2020, de YouTube: https://www.youtube.com/watch?v=xDE5SZyt7tw&feature=youtu.be

Colegio Blest Gana. (30 de Diciembre de 2012). *El Fenómeno de Finlandia - Educación.* Recuperado el 26 de Octubre de 2020, de YouTube: https://www.youtube.com/watch?v=nDXDrvd1utE&feature=youtu.be

Global Connection. (s.f.). *Educación en Casa o Homeschool.* Recuperado el 21 de Octubre de 2020, de Global Connection: https://www.estudieenelexterior.com.co/programas/educacion-en-casa

Macguire, E. (21 de Enero de 2016). *Jóvenes obtienen alquileres baratos en hogar de ancianos en Finlandia.* Recuperado el 20 de Octubre de 2020, de CNN: https://cnnespanol.cnn.com/2016/01/21/jovenes-obtienen-alquileres-baratos-en-hogar-de-ancianos-finlandes/

OIT. (s.f.). *¿Qué tan grande es la brecha salarial de género en su país?* Recuperado el 22 de Octubre de 2020, de Organización Internacional del Trabajo: https://www.ilo.org/global/about-the-ilo/multimedia/maps-and-charts/enhanced/WCMS_650872/lang--es/index.htm

OIT. (26 de Noviembre de 2018). *El crecimiento mundial del salario registra el nivel más bajo desde 2008 mientras que las mujeres todavía ganan 20 por ciento menos que los hombres.* Recuperado el 22 de Octubre de 2020, de Organización Internacional del Trabajo: https://www.ilo.org/global/about-the-ilo/mission-and-objectives/features/WCMS_650648/lang--es/index.htm

OMS. (Agosto de 2017). *10 datos sobre la lactancia materna.* Recuperado el 20 de Octubre de 2020, de Organización Mundial de la Salud: https://www.who.int/features/factfiles/breastfeeding/es/

OMS. (s.f.). *Lactancia materna.* Recuperado el 20 de Octubre de 2020, de Organización Mundial de la Salud: https://www.who.int/maternal_child_adolescent/topics/newborn/nutrition/breastfeeding/es/#:~:text=La%20leche%20materna%20promueve%20el,restablecimiento%20en%20caso%20de%20enfermedad

ONU. (s.f.). *17 objetivos para transformar nuestro mundo.* Recuperado el 22 de Octubre de 2020, de Organicación de las Naciones Unidas: https://www.un.org/sustainabledevelopment/es/

ONU. (s.f.). *La Declaración Universal de Derechos Humanos.* Recuperado el 23 de Octubre de 2020, de Organización de las Naciones Unidas: https://www.un.org/es/universal-declaration-human-rights/

OPS. (s.f.). *Beneficios de la lactancia materna*. Recuperado el 20 de Octubre de 2020, de Organización Panamericana de la Salud: https://www.paho.org/hq/index.php?option=com_content&view=article&id=9328:breastfeeding-benefits&Itemid=42403&lang=es

Reed, C. (5 de Abril de 2015). *Dutch nursing home offers rent-free housing to students*. Recuperado el 27 de Octubre de 2020, de PBS: https://www.pbs.org/newshour/world/dutch-retirement-home-offers-rent-free-housing-students-one-condition

Sanmartín, O. (16 de Febrero de 2015). *Educar sin escolarizar*. Recuperado el 22 de Octubre de 2020, de El Mundo: https://www.elmundo.es/espana/2015/02/16/54e0cf70e2704e6c038b4586.html

UNICEF. (s.f.). *Beneficios de la Lactancia materna*. Recuperado el 20 de Octubre de 2020, de UNICEF: https://www.unicef.org/Beneficios_de_la_Lactancia_Materna(1).pdf

Weaver, F. (Agosto de 2016). *Envejercer activamente es posible en Finlandia*. Recuperado el 27 de Octubre de 2020, de This is Finland: https://finland.fi/es/vida-y-sociedad/envejecer-activamente-es-posible-finlandia/

OTHER TITLES OF THE AUTHOR:

- "The Power of Self": Transforming your life, A look inside, mayo 2020
- El Poder del Ser, Transformando tu vida, una mirada interior, 2020, Mayo 2020
- Cartilla Planeación Estratégica desde el Ser Humano PEISH®, 2018,
- Una vida llena de amor, 2018, Autores: Maria Alexandra e Ivonne Stella Suárez-Rios.

www.ingramcontent.com/pod-product-compliance
Lightning Source LLC
Chambersburg PA
CBHW070246220526
45465CB00004B/1537